APR 2018

True Survival

ARON RALSTON

TRAPPED IN THE DESERT

Virginia Loh-Hagan

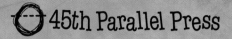

45th Parallel Press

Published in the United States of America by Cherry Lake Publishing
Ann Arbor, Michigan
www.cherrylakepublishing.com

Reading Adviser: Marla Conn MS, Ed., Literacy specialist, Read-Ability, Inc.
Book Designer: Felicia Macheske

Photo Credits: © Poprotskiy Alexey/Shutterstock.com, cover; © f11photo/Shutterstock.com, 5; © My Good Images/Shutterstock.com, 7; © Greg Epperson/Shutterstock.com, 8; © Paul W. Heaton/Shutterstock.com, 11; © Barakaphoto/Shutterstock.com, 12; © klaikungwon/Shutterstock.com, 15; © Kris Wiktor/Shutterstock.com, 17; © NadyaEugene/Shutterstock.com, 18; © Maria Jeffs/Shutterstock.com, 21; © EXTREME-PHOTOGRAPHER/iStock.com, 22; © s_bukley/Shutterstock.com, 25; © rdonar/Shutterstock.com, 27; © Sergey Lyashenko/Shutterstock.com, 28

Graphic Elements Throughout: © Gordan/Shutterstock.com; © adike/Shutterstock.com; © Yure/Shutterstock.com

45th Parallel Press is an imprint of Cherry Lake Publishing.

Library of Congress Cataloging-in-Publication Data

Names: Loh-Hagan, Virginia, author.
Title: Aron Ralston : trapped in the desert / by Virginia Loh-Hagan.
Description: Ann Arbor, Michigan : Cherry Lake Publishing, 2018. | Series:
 True survival | Includes bibliographical references and index.
Identifiers: LCCN 2017029640| ISBN 9781534107731 (hardcover)
| ISBN 9781534109711 (pdf) | ISBN 9781534108721 (pbk.) | ISBN 9781534120709
 (hosted ebook)
Subjects: LCSH: Rock climbing accidents—Utah—Bluejohn Canyon—Juvenile
 literature. | Ralston, Aron—Juvenile literature. | Desert
 survival—Utah—Bluejohn Canyon—Juvenile literature.
Classification: LCC GV199.42.U82 B585 2018 | DDC 796.522/30979254—dc23
LC record available at https://lccn.loc.gov/201702964

Cherry Lake Publishing would like to acknowledge the work of The Partnership for 21st Century Skills.
Please visit *www.p21.org* for more information.

Printed in the United States of America
Corporate Graphics

table of contents

chapter one

Rising and Falling

Who is Aron Ralston? What is canyoneering?

Aron Ralston was born on October 27, 1975. He was born in Marion, Ohio. He and his family moved to Denver, Colorado. He was 12 years old. Then he moved to Pittsburgh. He went to a university there. He studied **mechanical engineering**. This means he designs machines. He also studied French and piano.

He moved to Phoenix, Arizona. He worked as an engineer. He worked for a big company. Then he quit. He didn't want to work in an office. He wanted go on adventures. He wanted to be outside.

Ralston graduated from Carnegie Mellon University.

spotlight biography

Amber VanHecke got stranded. This happened in 2017. She was 24 years old. She was a college student in Texas. She went to the Grand Canyon. She went by herself. She posted her plans online. She was near the South Rim. She lost cell contact. She was lost. She ran out of gas. She was trapped for 5 days. She said, "I was panicking and crying and sobbing. I was a mess." She made a Help sign with rocks. She made a signal fire. She left notes. On the fifth day, she walked until her phone would work. She called 911. A helicopter rescued her. She had spent 119 hours alone in the desert.

He moved to Aspen, Colorado. He wanted to climb mountains. He had a goal. He wanted to climb Colorado's "fourteeners." These are mountains over 14,000 feet (4,267 meters) high. There are 59 of these mountains. He wanted to climb them by himself. This is called **solo-climbing**. He wanted to climb them in winter. This had never been done before. He achieved this goal in 2005.

Ralston also liked **canyoneering**. It means traveling in **canyons**. Canyons are clefts between mountains. They can be deep. They can be steep.

Climbing mountains in winter means there's snow.

Canyoneering is a sport. People do this in different ways. They walk. They scramble. They climb. They jump. They swim. They **rappel**. Rappel is using a rope to climb down something. People like to **descend** into canyons. Descend means to go down.

People like to canyoneer in **remote** places. Remote means far away from cities and people. People like to canyoneer in **rugged** places. Rugged means wild. Sometimes, canyoneering can be dangerous. People need special skills. They need to be able to **navigate**. Navigate means to find places.

◄ Rappelling takes a lot of practice to do safely.

chapter two

Trapped in Rock

Where did Ralston go? How did he get trapped?

Aron Ralston went to Bluejohn Canyon. This is in Canyonlands National Park in Utah. It is the desert. It took him 5 hours to drive there. He only planned to be gone 1 day.

He went hiking. He went alone. He explored **narrow** canyons. Narrow means tight spaces. He climbed. He made daring jumps. He used ropes.

He found a canyon. The drop was 10 feet (3 m). The canyon was 3 feet (1 m) wide. Ralston descended. He slipped and fell. He loosened a **boulder**. A boulder is a big rock. He made it move when he climbed over it. He didn't mean to do this.

Ralston was in the middle of nowhere.

The rock fell. Ralston put his hands up. He tried to protect himself. The rock smashed his left hand. It crushed his right arm against the canyon wall. His right hand and lower arm were stuck. Ralston was trapped against a rock.

He moved his feet. He was able to stand straight. But he couldn't free himself.

He was in trouble. He hadn't told anyone where he was going. No one would be coming to save him. This happened on April 26, 2003.

Ralston was stuck under 800 pounds (363 kilograms) of rock.

explained by
science

Getting trapped is scary. Scientists studied why some people survive and some don't. They found that survivors have certain characteristics. Survivors can put up with pain. They focus more on their mind than their body. Survivors have resilience. They can adapt, cope, and recover. They get over things. They don't quit. They're positive. They're flexible. They believe they can make it through. They have survival skills. They stay calm. They know how to solve problems. But bodies need food and water. Bodies change to save energy. People can live for more than 3 weeks without food. But they can only live a week without water. People will eventually die without food and water.

chapter three

Deep Cuts

What supplies did Ralston have? How did he survive? How did he get free?

Ralston had a small backpack. He had 34 ounces (1 liter) of water. He had 2 burritos. He had a few chocolate bits. He had headphones. He had a video camera. He had hiking boots. He had climbing gear. He had a **utility** tool. Utility means something that can be used for several things. This tool had a **dull** knife. Dull means not sharp. He didn't have a phone.

He had to make his food and water last. He slowly sipped. He slowly ate. He ate a little at a time.

He tried to free his arm. He tried to break the rock. He chipped away at it. He tried to lift the rock. He did this for 3 days. Nothing worked.

Ralston had bought a $15 flashlight. He got the utility tool for free.

would you?

- **Would you go canyoneering?** People like being outdoors. They like looking at the beautiful canyons. They like the thrill of canyoneering. But it can be dangerous. Canyons can have sharp, steep edges. They are far away from cities and people.

- **Would you drink your own pee?** Some people get trapped in places. They run out of water. They drink their own pee. They do this to stay alive. A healthy person's pee is 95 percent water and sterile. Sterile means pure. Some think it's safe to drink pee for a short time. But other organizations say not to drink it. They think it makes things worse.

Ralston knew he had to **amputate** his arm. Amputate means to cut off. He tested ways to tie up his arm. He needed to control the blood loss. He tested ways to cut his arm. He made light cuts. He needed to cut through bone. But he didn't have the correct tools.

He ran out of food and water. This happened on the fifth day. Ralston drank his own pee.

He thought he was going to die. He carved information on the canyon wall. He wrote his name. He wrote his birthday. He wrote the day he thought he'd die. He filmed good-bye to his family.

The nights were cold. Temperatures dropped to 30 degrees Fahrenheit (-1 degree Celsius).

He dreamed about his future son. This gave him hope. He fought to live. He had an idea. He hurled himself against the rock. This bent his arm. The rock snapped his bones.

He needed to cut through the skin. The knife pierced his skin. It rested on his bone. He cut. Gases came out. They smelled bad. His arm had already started to die. He stabbed instead of sawed. His arm was free. This took an hour.

Ralston was in pain. He was also happy. He was alive and free.

◄ Ralston's dream about his future family gave him the will to survive.

chapter four

Will to Live

How did he save himself? How was he saved?

Ralston was stuck for 5 days. He was stuck for 127 hours. He freed himself. He used his teeth and one arm to hold his climbing rope. He rappelled down 65 feet (20 m).

He walked 5 miles (8 km). He was bleeding. He'd lost 40 pounds (18 kg). He was weak. He ran into a Dutch family. They gave him food and water. They signaled for help.

Rescue helicopters are important for helping people in wild areas.

Ralston worked at an outdoor gear shop.

Ralston's family had called for help. They had reported him missing. They got worried when he didn't show up for work.

Rescue workers were looking for him. They traced his credit cards. They found his car. They tracked him. They were searching the area.

A helicopter saw Ralston and the Dutch family signaling for help. It took him to a hospital. The ride took 12 minutes. Rescue workers tried to keep Ralston awake. Ralston walked into the hospital by himself.

Ralston was saved 4 hours after cutting off his arm.

survival tips

SURVIVE IN THE WILD!

- Don't jump. Jumping injures lower legs. Bring a rope and use it.

- Be careful of steep cliffs. Watch edges especially when taking pictures.

- Stay on the trail.

- Check the weather. Avoid bad weather.

- Watch water levels. Heavy rains cause flash floods.

- Stay calm. Wait to be rescued. Listen for helicopters. Listen for other people.

- Signal by reflecting the sun off a mirror.

- Know how to tie knots.

- Don't make descents late in the day. Use the sunlight.

chapter five

Moving On

What happened to Ralston's arm?
What did Ralston do after his accident?

Park officials found Ralston's arm. They got it from under the rock. It took 13 men to do this. The men used special machines. They moved the rock. Only then could they get his arm.

His arm was **cremated**. Cremated means burned to ashes. The ashes were given to Ralston.

Ralston went back to the spot. He spread his ashes in the canyon. He said that's where they belong. He cried tears of joy. He was happy to be alive. He did this on his 28th birthday.

Ralston became famous. He was on television.

Rest in Peace

Keyhole Canyon is in Zion National Park. It's in Utah. It's popular with hikers. A group of hikers went there. This happened in 2015. There were 7 hikers. Their names were Don Teichner, Steve and Linda Arthur, Robin Brum, Muku Reynolds, Gary Favela, and Mark MacKenzie. They descended deep into the canyon. They shared a single rope. Then, there was a storm. There were heavy rains. This caused a flash flood. The 7 hikers got swept away. They died. Three days later, rescuers found all their bodies. A family member said, "They cared about the wilderness. And they knew how powerful it can be."

Ralston had to cut his arm off. He did it at the right time. The arm was already beginning to die. If he'd cut his arm off earlier, he would've bled to death. If he didn't cut off his arm, he would've died in the canyon.

He got a fake arm. He helps people with disabilities. He gives them gear. He provides opportunities. He wants people to climb.

He changed his life. He had to use his left hand more. For example, he learned to type with one hand. Playing piano helped him. It made his left hand strong.

Ralston helps protect nature.

Ralston didn't quit. He climbed again. His first climb was 2 months later. But it took him 4 years to get as good as he had been.

He travels around the world. He climbs mountains. He still climbs by himself. He wants to climb all the highest peaks. He climbed Denali by himself. Denali is North America's highest mountain. He also likes water sports. He rafted through the Grand Canyon.

Ralston wanted to live. He fought for his life.

◄ Ralston has taken more than 100 river trips.

Did You Know?

- Canyoneering started in Europe. It started in the 1970s.

- There's a movie about Ralston. It's called *127 Hours*. James Franco plays Ralston. Ralston said the film is "so factually accurate, it is as close to a documentary as you can get and still be a drama." The movie was filmed at the exact spot of Ralston's accident.

- Ralston filmed his ordeal. But he said he'd never show it in public.

- Bluejohn Canyon is near Robbers Roost. This is where Butch Cassidy hid. Cassidy was a famous outlaw. He lived during the days of the Wild West.

- Ralston is an experienced outdoorsman. He said, "I was accustomed to being in far, far riskier environments. So, I thought going into that canyon was a walk in the park. There were no avalanches. It was a beautiful day. And I was essentially just walking." He didn't expect to get trapped. He'd had more dangerous trips.

- He cut a nerve in his arm. He described the nerve as "a piece of extra-thick spaghetti." He snapped it. He described it as "plucking a guitar string."

- This wasn't Ralston's first accident. He had gone skiing with 2 friends. They were caught in an avalanche. Avalanches are when snow flows quickly down a mountain. They're dangerous. Ralston almost died.

Consider This!

Take a Position: Canyoneering is fun. But it also impacts the land. People drill holes. They leave tools behind. Do you think people should be allowed to go canyoneering? Argue your point with reasons and evidence.

Say What? Read the Nailed It series from 45th Parallel Press books. These books are about extreme sports. For example, read *Rock Climbing* and *Mountain Climbing*. Why do people like to do extreme sports? Explain the pros and cons of extreme sports.

Think About It! Watch *127 Hours*. How well did this movie stick to the facts? What parts were made up? Why did the moviemakers add those parts?

Learn More

- Baxter, Roberta. *Aron Ralston: Pinned in a Canyon*. Mankato, MN: Childs World, 2016.
- Doeden, Matt. *Trapped in a Canyon! Aron Ralston's Story of Survival*. Mankato, MN: Edge Books, 2007.

Glossary

amputate (AM-pyuh-tate) to cut off

boulder (BOHL-dur) big rock

canyoneering (kan-yuhn-EER-ing) the sport of traveling in canyons by swimming, hiking, rappelling, or other means

canyons (KAN-yuhnz) clefts between mountains

cremated (KREE-mayt-id) burned to ashes

descend (dih-SEND) to go down

dull (DUHL) not sharp

mechanical engineering (muh-KAN-ih-kuhl en-juh-NEER-ing) profession of designing, making, and operating machines

narrow (NAR-oh) tight space

navigate (NAV-ih-gate) to find something

rappel (ruh-PEL) using rope to climb down

remote (rih-MOHT) far away

rugged (RUHG-id) rough, wild, dangerous

solo-climbing (SOH-loh KLIME-ing) climbing by oneself

utility (yoo-TIL-ih-tee) being useful and functional

Index

About the Author

Dr. Virginia Loh-Hagan is an author, university professor, former classroom teacher, and curriculum designer. She always lets people know where she is at all times. She's afraid of going missing without anyone knowing. She lives in San Diego with her very tall husband and very naughty dogs. To learn more about her, visit www.virginialoh.com.